DISCOVERING

MALAYSIA

By Richard Balkwill

A ZOË BOOK

A ZOË BOOK

© 1997 Zoë Books Limited

Devised and produced by
Zoë Books Limited
15 Worthy Lane
Winchester
Hampshire SO23 7AB
England

First published in Great Britain in 1997 by
Zoë Books Limited
15 Worthy Lane
Winchester
Hampshire SO23 7AB

A record of the CIP data is available from the British Library.

ISBN 1 874488 91 6

Printed in Italy by Grafedit SpA
Design and Production: Sterling Associates
Map: Sterling Associates
Picture research: Manda Joyce

Photographic acknowledgments

The publishers wish to acknowledge, with thanks, the following photographic sources:

Cover: Impact/Richard McCaig; Title page: NHPA/Andy Rouse; 5l Impact Photos/David Palmer; 5r The Hutchison Library/Jon Burbank; 6 Impact Photos/Alain Evrard; 7l NHPA/Norbert Wu; 7r NHPA/Morten Strange; 8 The Hutchison Library/Nick Owen; 9l The Hutchison Library/Nick Haslam; 9r NHPA/Martin Harvey; 10,11l Impact Photos/Mark Henley; 11r Impact Photos/Alain Evrard; 12 Impact Photos/Piers Cavendish; 13l The Hutchison Library/Angela Silvertop; 13r The Hutchison Library/R.House; 14 The Hutchison Library/Jon Burbank; 15l Impact Photos/Julian Calder; 15r Impact Photos/Mark Henley; 16 Impact Photos/Piers Cavendish; 17l The Hutchison Library/Juliet Highet; 17r The Hutchison Library/R.Ian Lloyd; 18 NHPA/B.Jones & M.Shimlock; 19l NHPA/Michael Tweedie; 19r NHPA/Pavel German; 20 The Hutchison Library/Jon Burbank; 21l Impact Photos/Mark Henley; 21r Impact Photos/Anita Corbin; 22 Impact Photos/Alain Evrard; 23l Impact Photos Mark Henley; 23r Impact Photos/Alain Evrard; 24,25l The Hutchison Library/R.Ian Lloyd; 25r Impact Photos/Dominic Sansoni; 26,27l AKG London, 27r Mary Evans Picture Library; 28 AKG London; 29l The Hutchison Library R.Ian Lloyd; 29r Impact Photos/Christophe Bluntzer

The publishers have made every effort to trace the copyright holders, but if they have inadvertently overlooked any, they will be pleased to make the necessary arrangement at the first opportunity.

Cover: *Central Kuala Lumpur*

Title page: *A clouded leopard*

Editorial note
The place names and spellings in this book are those in current use. Sometimes, an older name might be more familiar to readers. In this case, we give both versions of the name on first use – for example, Melaka (Malacca).

Contents

4

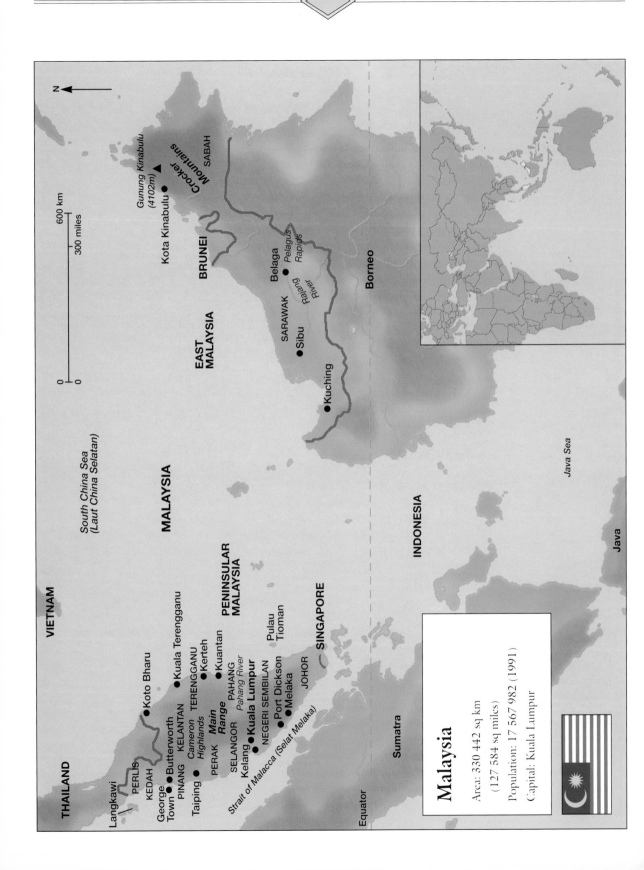

Selamat datang!

Welcome to Malaysia – a modern country with a rich and varied past. Malaysia has two separate parts. There is Peninsular Malaysia, with Thailand to the north and Singapore at its Southern tip, and East Malaysia. The two main areas of East Malaysia – Sabah and Sarawak – are part of an island to the east.

Traders and settlers

For thousands of years, sea travellers from all over Asia have passed by, traded and settled in the land we now call Malaysia. Merchants traded in the land's rich natural wealth, such as rubber and oil. When people from Europe came to live there, they took over, or colonized, parts of Malaysia. Their systems of government were not always fair to the Malaysian people. Today, Malaysia is an independent

Sunset on the island of Pulau Tioman

Special cakes for a Chinese festival

country where people vote for their government.

Many travellers and settlers brought traditions and cultures which still exist in Malaysia. Malay, Chinese, Indian, Arab and European people live there. There are also descendants of the earliest peoples – the Orang Asli of Peninsular Malaysia, and the tribal peoples of East Malaysia.

Malaysia is a country of contrasts. It is a tropical paradise with many white, sandy beaches and a deep blue sea. Two-thirds of the country is covered in thick rainforest. Malaysia is also highly industrialized. Steel and oil refining are important Malaysian industries.

Peninsular Malaysia

Peninsular Malaysia is sometimes known as West Malaysia. Melaka, one of the 13 states of Malaysia, is in the south west of Peninsular Malaysia. The city of Melaka (originally spelt Malacca), is the oldest in Malaysia.

North of Melaka is the state of Negeri Sembilan. At Port Dickson, there are elegant tourist beaches as well as a large oil refinery. Further north is the state of Perak. The city of Taiping was once an important mining centre.

The island state of Pinang is connected to the west coast by the longest toll bridge in Asia. You can take the funicular railway up Pinang Hill and get a good view over George Town, the state capital. Chinese settlers built splendid mansions and temples there.

Further north is the state of Kedah. It is known as the rice bowl of Malaysia because crops grow well there.

The east coast

The northernmost state in the east of Peninsular Malaysia is Kelantan. From the state capital, Kota Bharu, you can visit small islands and wonderful beaches where turtles lay their eggs. People in Kota Bharu still make

The Cheng Hoon Teng Temple, Melaka, is Malaysia's oldest temple. It was built in 1646.

A turtle covers her newly-laid eggs with sand.

traditional craftwork in silver and batik. There is also some industry, such as boat-building.

In the state of Terengganu, Kerteh is a centre for the oil and natural gas industry. Workers live in flats provided by the company. Big canteens serve local food all day.

The Pahang river is the longest river in Peninsular Malaysia. It flows 436 kilometres (271 miles) to the sea. In the villages along the river, fishing families live in boats or in small houses built on stilts over the water. The state that the river flows through is also called Pahang. Its capital, Kuantan, is the centre of the oil palm industry.

The oil is used in making soap, lubricants and foods. Only a few kilometres from Kuantan is the old royal capital of Pahang Pekan.

Among the jungle-covered hills of Pahang is a group of lakes called Tasek Chini. Legend says that the lakes drowned an ancient walled city. Off the coast of Pahang is the beautiful island of Pulau Tioman.

Taman Negara National Park

Taman Negara is the largest national park in Malaysia. It is in the middle of Peninsular Malaysia, in the Main Range of mountains. The highest mountain in Peninsular Malaysia is in Taman Negara park. It is called Gunung Tahan and it rises to 2187 metres (7175 feet). Malaysian people and foreign tourists visit the park all year round.

Rainforest in Taman Negara National Park

East Malaysia

East Malaysia is sometimes known as Island Malaysia because it is part of the island of Borneo. Borneo is the third-largest island in the world. It is about 400 kilometres (250 miles) to the east of Peninsular Malaysia. Borneo is divided between different countries. There are two Malaysian states, Sarawak and Sabah, on the island. There is also the country of Brunei, and part of the country of Indonesia.

The peaks of Mount Kinabulu at dawn

Sarawak

Sarawak is the largest state in Malaysia, Much of it is dense rainforest, in which the valuable hardwood *belian* grows.

The capital of Sarawak is Kuching. To the east of Kuching is the Rajang River, at 563 kilometres (350 miles), the longest in Malaysia. Near the town of Belaga the river races over the seven Pelagus Rapids. Each one has a name, such as Nabau ('python') and Rapoh ('grave').

Traders beside the Rajang River, the longest in Malaysia

Sabah

Sabah is in the north east of the island of Borneo. It was once known as the British North Borneo Company and was a centre of trade. Now traders mostly sell souvenirs for visiting tourists. Many different peoples live in this state, including the Bajau sea gypsies who live on the coast.

Sabah's capital city is Kota Kinabulu, once known as Jesselton. The name Kota Kinabulu means 'sacred home of the dead'. The name was given to the area by the Kadazan tribe, the largest group of native people in Sabah.

The Crocker mountain range rises to its highest point at Mount Kinabulu (*Gunung Kinabulu* in the Malaysian language). The summit of Mount Kinabulu is called Low's Peak. At 4102 metres (13 455 feet) above sea level it is the highest place in the whole of Malaysia.

The islands east of Sabah form the Tunku Abdul Rahman National Park. It is a paradise of coral reefs, clear water and white sandy beaches. Local people and visitors from all over the world come to the park.

Creatures great and small

Mount Kinabulu is part of a vast national park with many different landscapes – from thick mangrove on the coast, up to cloud forests and flowery meadows. The park is home to a wonderful variety of wildlife. There are birds such as hornbills, insects such as the Atlas Moth (25 centimetres (10 inches) long !), and tiny mammals such as the lori (a lemur) and the tarsier (similar to a lemur).

The giant Atlas Moth

Kuala Lumpur

Kuala Lumpur is the capital of Malaysia. It is inland, on the west side of Peninsular Malaysia. About 135 years ago, Kuala Lumpur was just forest and swamp, where two rivers, the Kelang and the Gombak, met. *Kuala Lumpur* means 'muddy place where rivers flow together'. Chinese traders set up a shop there for the tin miners at Ampang. Before long, Kuala Lumpur grew into a shanty town serving the tin trade.

In the 1860s, the Chinese and British joined together to improve the city buildings. A railway was built in 1886 to connect Kuala Lumpur to the port of Kelang 64 kilometres (40 miles) away. Later, people who had made money from tin mining built fine, large houses in Kuala Lumpur.

The Sultan Abdul Samad building, Kuala Lumpur, lit at night

A peanut seller in KL's Chinatown

Today, 1.2 million people live in KL, as Kuala Lumpur is sometimes called. KL is still growing fast as more and more people go there to find work. Many people live in flats in high-rise apartment buildings, or other modern houses equipped with televisions, hi-fi and washing machines.

There are also older, more crowded areas in Kuala Lumpur, such as Chinatown. Chinatown is lively and noisy. Traders set up market and food stalls in the early morning, and stay open late into the night. Local people shop for vegetables and fruit, meat and fresh fish, alongside tourists looking for a bargain.

Steel pinnacles

Kuala Lumpur is a centre for business and telecommunications. Companies from around the world have offices there. The world's tallest building (in 1997), Petronas Towers, is in Kuala Lumpur. It is 452 metres (1483 feet) high.

Sights to see

Kuala Lumpur has many fine buildings. **The Masjid Jamek mosque** was completed in 1907 and is made of pale pink bricks.

The Sultan Abdul Samad building is the legal high court in Malaysia. Built in 1894, it has onion-shaped copper domes and a high clock tower.

There are colourful markets, such as the **Pasar Seni**, or **Central Market**, where you can buy arts and crafts from Malaysia and neighbouring countries.

The Lake Gardens, is where you can picnic and go boating on the lake. You can also see the Gardens' collection of orchids. The collection contains over 800 species.

People travel from the suburbs where they live, to the centre of the city where they work. Some use buses, cars or motorcycles. Others cycle to avoid the terrible traffic jams. Traffic noise and pollution are problems in Kuala Lumpur, as in other cities of the world.

Orchids in the Lake Gardens' collection

Where people live

About half of all people in Malaysia live in the countryside, and about half in cities and towns. This is different from most other countries, where most people live in cities and towns. Kuala Lumpur is the only big city in Malaysia. Outside the capital city, the pace of life is much slower.

Malaysian houses are usually made of wood and bamboo. Sometimes they are decorated with wooden carvings. Many old towns, such as Melaka and Kuching, also have houses and buildings from the Portuguese, Dutch or British colonial times.

Beside rivers and near the coast, people build houses on stilts over the water. You might have to cross a covered footbridge to go in, or to go from one part of the house to another. Large windows let in as much air and light as possible. The roofs are sometimes made of thatch.

The Murut people usually build their large longhouses near water. Everyone lives together in the communal longhouse.

This family lives in the countryside, in a wooden house on stilts.

A sense of peace

Deep in the country, in clearings in the thick forest, you will find some Malay people's ideal way of life. *Kampongs*, or hamlets, are small groups of houses where people live according to Muslim tradition. They cook before dawn, carry out household tasks or work on small plots of land during the day and return indoors in the evening. The sun sets towards Mecca and people go to pray at the local temple, the mosque.

A peaceful, slower lifestyle is said to lead to the state of mind most Malays aim for – *senang*. The word means happiness which comes from a feeling of being at ease with yourself.

In remote parts of Sarawak and Sabah, some people live in caves. The Punan people are cave-dwellers in the Mount Mulu National Park. Other people move from place to place, leading a nomadic life. They use darts from wooden blowpipes to kill animals for food.

A fishing village in Terengganu

A bed for the night

Outside towns, rest houses have been built where local or foreign travellers may stay. There is one in the Cameron Highlands called 'Ye Old Smokehouse'. It looks very old, but was built in mock-Tudor style in the 1920s.

The Smokehouse, a 'home from home' for Britons in Malaysia

Peoples and languages

Many people call Malaysia a 'mini-Asia' because people from so many different countries live there. The local Malay population is sometimes called *bumiputra*. It makes up about 59 per cent of the total population of over 17 million.

Chinese people make up about a third of the population

The second largest group – 32 per cent – are of Chinese or Cantonese origin. They came mainly from southern China. About 9 per cent are Indian. Many of them came from the south of India as workers or slaves. They worked in the tin mines, and later in rubber plantations. In the cities, people of all races now live and work together.

The religions practised in Malaysia are as varied as the people. In Melaka, there is a street where a Muslim mosque, a Hindu temple and a Chinese Taoist Buddhist temple are next to each other. There are many other traditional faiths.

In the countryside, the ways of life of different peoples remain separate. In Sarawak, the Iban tribe live in longhouses near the rivers around Kuching and Sibu. Further upstream, on the Rajang River, are the Kenyah and Kayan people. Their languages and traditions are different, yet both tribes are skilful sailors who can steer a boat through dangerous rapids. The Kelabit people grow rice in the hills.

In Sabah, the Kadazan people live around Mount Kinabulu. They are hill or terrace farmers, and they make many beautiful things out of bamboo.

A Kelabit couple in Sarawak

Newspapers in Chinese (left), Malaysian (middle) and Roman (right) print

Languages

Most people in Malaysia speak the Bahasa Malaysia language, also called Malay. It has its own alphabet, although most street signs are written in the Roman alphabet (the one used in this book). Mandarin and Chinese dialects are also spoken. The main Indian language is Tamil. English is also widely understood, except in the remote country areas.

Some Malay phrases
Selamat pagi – 'good morning'
Apa khatar? –'how are you?'
Terima kasih – 'thank you'

People at work

Building cars on an assembly line in the Proton car factory

In the cities, people work in industries that produce cars, electronic equipment, chemicals, steel and clothes. In the country, people grow crops such as rice and tea. Fishing is also an important source of income.

About 150 years ago, people began to need more and more tin. It was used to make cans for food. The city of Kuala Lumpur grew up very quickly because deposits of tin were found nearby at Ampang in the 1850s and 1860s. Malaysia is still the biggest tin exporter in the region.

Since 1980, Malaysia's main crop has been palm oil. The oil is extracted from the kernels of the ornamental palm tree. This type of palm did not grow naturally in Malaysia. It was introduced from West Africa in 1875.

Malaysia exports more rubber than any other country in the world. The first rubber trees were grown there in the 1880s. They were introduced by

Picking tea on a tea plantation

H N Ridley who took the seeds from rubber trees growing by the River Amazon in Brazil. The climate in the two places was similar, and the plants grew well. Within 20 years, trees producing latex, the liquid sap from which rubber is made, were growing all over the Malay peninsula.

Oil and gas

In recent years, Malaysia's most important natural resources have been oil and gas. Most of this comes from under the sea. Oil was first discovered off the coast of Sarawak in 1910. Later, in 1978, oil and natural gas were discovered in large amounts under the sea near Kuala Terengganu.

Aiming for development

Since 1990, the National Development Policy has aimed to make Malaysia a fully-developed industrial country by the year 2020. Malaysia hopes to earn as much from exporting its goods to sell to other countries as it pays to buy imported goods from abroad.

Travelling around

Malaysia has always been well connected to the rest of the world. Today, Malaysian Airlines planes take people from one part of Malaysia to another, or to Europe and Australia. The railway from Singapore, through Kuala Lumpur and Butterworth, north to the border with Thailand, carries a lot of freight and some tourists. Outside the cities, the roads are twisting and slow.

Industries old and new – a fishing boat passes an oil depot

Climate and wildlife

Malaysia is very near the Equator. The climate is hot and humid. The temperature is always between 20°C and 30°C, except in the cool highlands and at the tops of mountains. Malaysia is sometimes called 'the land where the winds meet' – the monsoon winds blow from the northeast between November and March, and from the southwest between June and October. About 250 centimetres (nearly 100 inches) of rain fall every year, mostly during the northeast monsoon.

The orang–utan is an endangered species.

People wear loose clothes to keep cool. Women wear sarongs made of silk or other light cloth and men wear short-sleeved shirts. No-one needs a sweater, but most people have an umbrella.

Plants grow very quickly in this climate and much of Malaysia is covered by thick, green forests. The forest is home to a huge variety of animals and plants.

Orang-utans – the name means 'forest person' – are apes with orange-red fur. They have become very rare. There are tigers, leopards and

The Rafflesia *– the world's largest flower*

elephants in Malaysia, but it is unusual to see them in the wild. Deer and monkeys are common, but you are more likely to hear them than to see them.

Giants of nature

Malaysia also has many types of reptile. There are king cobras, which are poisonous, and pythons up to 10 metres (more than 30 feet) long. There are also lizards, such as the small and harmless gecko.

Malaysia's forests are full of the noise and colour of birds and insects. There are some very large butterflies and moths. The Rajah Brooke Birdwing has a wingspan of up to 18 centimetres (7 inches). In the many caves of Malaysia, you will find bats. Millions of them live in just one cave in Mulu National Park.

Malaysia is famous for its orchids. A strange plant called the *Rafflesia* also grows there. Its bud can take over a year to blossom, and then the flower lasts for just a few days. The *Rafflesia* has the world's largest flower. The petals are sometimes over 90 centimetres (3 feet) wide.

The fastest-growing tree in the world is found in the Malaysian forests. It is called *albizzia falcataria*. It can grow 10 metres (35 feet) in just over a year.

An insect-eating plant

Pitcher plants are shaped like a jug or deep bowl. They fill with rainwater which mixes with the plant's nectar, attracting insects. The insects fall in and are slowly digested by the plant.

The nectar-filled pitcher plant, tempting insects to their doom!

Food and drink

The food in Malaysia is very varied – new dishes have been introduced by the different peoples who settled there. You can find the best Malay, Chinese, Indian and Thai cooking.

People eat a good breakfast and usually have a family meal early in the evening. Lunch is often a snack. At weekends the family eats together in the middle of the day.

The staple food is rice, although noodles are also popular. Many spices are used in Malay cooking – coriander and ginger give food a warm, sweetish taste, lemongrass gives a lemony, sour flavour and chilli pepper makes things taste hot. Some dishes are delicately flavoured with lemon and coconut. Coconut trees are common in Malaysia, and the milk from the nut, called *santan*, is used in soups and curries. Desserts are often very sweet.

Chinese dishes laid out for a festival

Eating a 'steamboat'

One famous dish is called 'steamboat'. People dip pieces of fish and other seafoods into a bowl of boiling stock which is set in the middle of the table.

Satay is a common Malaysian dish, which is found all over the world. Pieces of grilled meat are served with a sauce made from peanuts. Pork is not eaten because the Muslim faith, which is followed by many Malaysians, forbids it.

Vegetables and fruits

Many kinds of vegetable and tropical fruit grow in Malaysia. Aubergines, sweet potatoes, lentils and okra (ladies' fingers) are used in vegetable curries. You can buy vegetables, fruit and

A selection of local fruits and vegetables in Kota Bharu market, Kelantan

These children are having their breakfast at nursery school.

cooked food at stalls along the road. People sometimes use a banana leaf as a plate.

The national fruit of Malaysia is the rambutan. Inside its prickly, reddish skin, is a soft, white fruit. It tastes similar to a lychee. Melon, pineapple, papaya, guava and mango are common and there are 40 different kinds of banana in Malaysia.

Favourite drinks

Fruit juice drinks, especially those made from mango, starfruit, guava or lime, are popular. Children also like soya bean milk served in a bag with a straw, or water flavoured with coconut.

People also drink tea, coffee, beer and wine. Malaysians in Sarawak drink a rice wine called *tuak*, which can be very strong.

Having fun

Malaysian people play many international sports, such as badminton and tennis. They also have their own type of volleyball, or aerial soccer, which is called *sepak teraw*. Players are not allowed to touch the ball (made of rattan) with their hands or arms.

Another traditional sport is *silat*, a martial art of self-defence. People wrestle with each other, or fence using a type of sword called a *kris*.

In Kelantan and Terengganu, there is an old tradition of kite-flying. The huge kites are up to 2 metres (over 6 feet) long and can fly at heights of 150 metres (500 feet). They are made of bamboo, covered in cloth to look like animals, fish or birds. People compete in kite fights.

Gasing, or top-spinning, is a popular Malay pastime. The top is like a large plate, with lead edges and a steel centre. Once the top has been set spinning, it is lifted on to a wooden post. It can go on spinning for up to two hours. Teams from villages compete to see how long they can make their top spin.

People have been flying kites in Malaysia for about 400 years.

A performance of Silat, *accompanied by drummers.*

Special days

The variety of religious beliefs in Malaysia means that there are many holidays and festivals during the year. People observe different holy days, according to their religion. During the Muslim festival of Hari Raya Puasa, families visit each other, bringing little gifts for the children.

At Christmas and New Year, many people take their main holiday. They go to the beach and have parties. Chinese New Year is celebrated in January or February. Families hold a three-day 'open house' when friends of all religions can visit.

Other special days include the Hindu festival of lights, known as Deepavali, and Malaysia's National Day (31st August).

Keeping a balance

Malaysia has such a long coastline that most Malaysians can go swimming and diving in their spare time. There are also many national parks to visit. Tourists come from all over the world to enjoy the beauty of Malaysia. The tourist industry makes an important contribution to the wealth of the country. But if too many visitors come, they could spoil the beautiful places they have come to see. Malaysia has to keep a balance between the two needs.

Schoolchildren celebrating Malaysia's National Day.

Arts and crafts

Malaysian arts and crafts are ancient and varied. Stone Age cave paintings, pottery and beads, believed to be over 40 000 years old, have been found in Sarawak.

Batik came originally from the Malay kingdom of Java and is now found all over Malaysia. A design of melted wax is put on to cloth, which is then dipped into dyes of different colours to make beautiful patterns. The cloth is sometimes made into a sarong or other clothes. Wedding dresses and other ceremonial clothes are often decorated with a brocade called *kain songket*. The brocade is made from threads of gold or silver woven into silk.

Using plants

Plants such as bamboo and palm are used to make thatched roofs, mats, screens, baskets and other household articles. In Sarawak, skilled weavers continue the old tradition of dyeing thread with natural dyes from plants. The threads are woven into hangings.

Painting a batik design in Terengganu

Metalwork

Malaysian people have been making things from silver and pewter for many years, especially in Perak. Pewter is made from tin mixed with antimony or copper to harden it. Silver boxes and pewter tankards can be found in markets all over Malaysia.

Graceful dances

There are many traditional dances in Malaysia. The men and women dancers do not touch each other at all during the dance. Some dances are based on historical events, while others tell the story of everyday activities, such as planting rice or harvesting crops.

A dancer in traditional costume and theatrical make-up

Behind the scenes at a shadow-puppet show

Some old court dances are still performed, such as the 'Candle Dance' which dates from the 15th century.

Shadows on a screen

Shadow-puppet plays were a common sight, before cinema and television arrived. They are still performed. The puppets are made of animal skin on bamboo sticks. They are moved behind a white cloth screen, with an oil lamp providing the light to cast the shadows. The stories are usually from the Hindu religion, and are accompanied by a traditional orchestra – drums, cymbals, gongs and a *serunai* (a type of oboe).

Malaysia's beginnings

We know people have been living in Malaysia for many thousands of years – a 40 000 year-old human skull has been found in caves in Sarawak. Archaeologists have also found Stone Age remains, over 30 000 years old, in Sabah and Perak. About 5000 years ago, settlers came from China and Tibet. Some of them were nomadic, while others stayed in one place, farming, fishing and hunting.

Traders from India arrived in Malaysia about 2000 years ago. They were looking for the 'Land of Gold'. Four hundred years later, Chinese merchants came in search of wealth.

By the 1400s, Melaka (Malacca) had become the largest and strongest state. At that time, Egypt controlled the spice routes to Europe, and only Muslim shipping was allowed to pass. So the rulers of Melaka converted from the Hindu to the Muslim faith.

Plan of Melaka under Portuguese control in the early 1600s

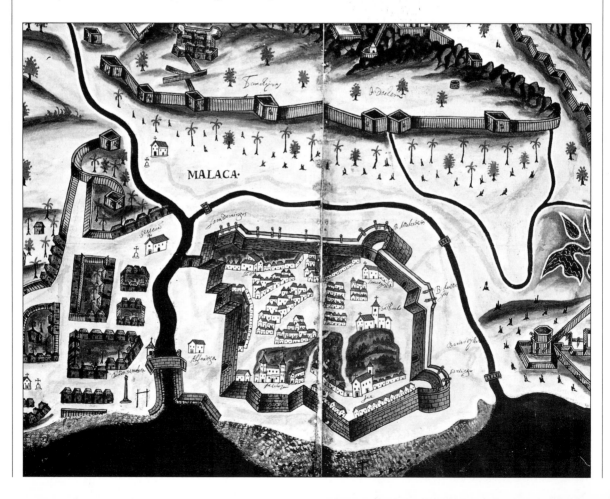

Vasco da Gama, shown here in India on his travels to secure trade routes for Portugal

European rulers

Vasco da Gama was a Portuguese sailor who first sailed round the southern tip of Africa in 1497. He then travelled on to India. The Portuguese wanted a bigger share of the spice trade from this route. In 1511, they attacked Melaka and took over the city. Later, the Dutch wanted to control Melaka. They fought and defeated the Portuguese in 1641. The Portuguese and Dutch brought the Christian religion to Malaysia.

In the 1700s, the British started to come to Malaysia as traders. They were already trading in tea from China, and needed a safe base on the route to Britain. In 1786, Francis Light set up a small British settlement in Pinang. The British influence became stronger when Thomas Stamford Raffles took over the port of Singapore in 1819.

A few years later, the British and Dutch reached an agreement on how the land that they each wanted should be divided up. Pinang, Melaka and Singapore became Britain's Straits Settlement. The land was divided to suit the colonists' needs, and did not pay much attention to where groups of the native people lived, or what languages they spoke.

'White Rajas'

In 1841, an Englishman called James Brooke helped the Raja of Brunei. In return he was given Sarawak and became its 'White Raja'. James was the first of three generations of Brookes to rule Sarawak. In 1963, Sarawak joined Malaysia.

Independence

British rule lasted in the Malay peninsula, and in Sarawak and North Borneo for about 100 years. In 1941, during the Second World War, the Japanese invaded and pushed out the British. After the war, the British returned. They tried to strengthen their rule by joining their old colonies together into a Malayan Union or a Federation of Malaya. Several groups, especially the Chinese, were against this. There was bitter fighting in the late 1940s. In the 1950s the Chinese formed a link with the Malays called the Alliance. By 1955 most people supported this, and independence followed in 1957.

The first Prime Minister, Tunku Abdul Rahman, proposed a Federation of Malaysia which was to include Malaya, Sarawak, North Borneo, Singapore and Brunei. The federation was set up in 1963, but Brunei did not join, and Singapore left in 1965. At first, nearby countries claimed that Sarawak and Sabah should not be part of the union. These claims were dropped after the death of their strongest spokesman, President Sukarno of Indonesia, in 1966.

A British aeroplane captured by Japanese soldiers in Malaysia in 1941, during the Second World War.

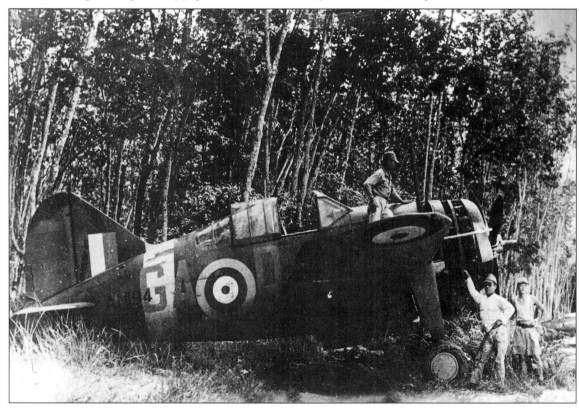

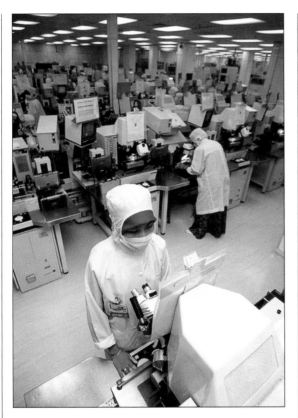

Manufacturing electronic circuits, Kuala Lumpur

New industries, new partners

In Malaysia today, Prime Minister Dr Mahathir Mohamed has tried to increase the country's trade with other parts of the world. The car and steel industries have grown quickly. Oil and palm oil are now more important than rubber and tin, which made the country's fortune in the early years of the 20th century.

Malaysia has formed alliances, such as ASEAN (a trading agreement), with other partners in the region. Dr Mohamed, sometimes called 'the business person's Prime Minister', has developed a 'Look East' policy. It

Green Malaysia

Plants and wildlife face extinction in Malaysia, as in many other countries. But as people become aware of the need for preservation, some industries are being more careful with natural resources.

encourages trade with neighbours such as Thailand and nearby Korea, rather than with the old European partners.

New hospitals have been built and young people receive a good education. Most Malaysian people have benefitted from the country's wealth and now have a good standard of living.

Young Malaysian schoolchildren

Fact file

Government

Malaysia is a democracy, where all adults have a vote. The head of state is a monarch called the *Yang di-Pertuan Agong*. The monarch is elected every five years by the rulers of some of the Malaysian states, from among themselves. The Prime Minister and a cabinet advise the monarch.

Each state has an elected government and a governor. There is also a central parliament called the *Majlis*. It consists of a 180-member House of Representatives, elected for five years, and a 70-member Senate. The Senate has 30 members elected by the Malaysian states, and 40 members chosen by the monarch.

Flag

The Malaysian flag has 14 horizontal stripes in red and white. They represent the 13 states and the federal government. On the left, at the top, is a dark blue panel with a yellow sun and a crescent moon. These are symbols of Islam, Malaysia's national religion.

National anthem

The country's national anthem is called *Negara Ku*.

Religion

About 53 per cent of the population are Muslims, who follow the faith of Islam. Hinduism, Buddhism and Christianity are also widespread and some of the Chinese population follow Confucianism. Some tribal peoples follow their own religion.

Money

The unit of currency is the Malaysian dollar (M$), called the *Ringgit*. This is made up of 100 *sen* (cents). There are coins from 1 to 50 cents, and notes from M$1 to M$1000.

Education

School is free, and compulsory for children aged 6 to 14. Lessons may be taught in Bahasa Malaysia, Chinese or Tamil (an Indian language). Bahasa Malaysia and English are compulsory subjects in all schools. Many pupils stay on until they are 18. They may then go on to study at one of the 16 universities and polytechnics.

Newspapers and television

The main newspaper in the Bahasa Malaysia language are the *Berita Harian* and *Utusan Malaysia*. There are English-language papers too, such as the *New Straits Times*.

Radio Television Malaysia is the government-run broadcasting service. There are six radio stations, and two television channels.There is a third, commercial channel, called TV Tiga.

Some famous people

Muzaffar Shah (Sultan of Malacca 1446-59) established Islam as the state religion

Vasco da Gama (1460-1524) was a Portuguese sailor who opened up trade routes

Saint Francis Xavier (1506-52) was a Roman Catholic missionary who established the first school in Melaka

Afonso de Albuquerque (1453-1515) took over Melaka in 1511 as part of Portugal's strategy for controlling trade routes

Colonel Francis Light (1740-94) was a British adventurer who set up a trading base in Pinang

Sir Thomas Stamford Bingley Raffles (1781-1826) worked for the East India Company and established the port of Singapore

Margaret Brooke wrote an account of British colonial life in Sarawak (published in 1913)

Tunku Abdul Rahman (1903-90) was the first Prime Minister of independent Malaysia

Dutuk Seri Dr Mahathir bin Mohamed (1925-) has been Prime Minister since 1981 and has done much to increase the country's prosperity

Hajah Rahman Osman (1939-) is a politician and businesswoman

Dato Seri Pakuda Rafidah Aziz (1943-) is Minister for International Trade and Industry. She speaks at many international conferences

Some key events in history

40 000 BC People were living in caves in Sarawak

3000 BC settlers came from China and Tibet. They were ancestors of today's Orang Asli people

c 300 BC Malay peoples arrived, probably from Indonesia

c 100 BC Indian traders arrived

c AD 1400 Srivijayan Prince Parameswara set up a trading base in the small fishing village of Melaka

1511 Portuguese took control of the state of Melaka. The Malay sultan moved south to Johor

1824 Anglo-Dutch treaty signed, dividing the land between the two countries

1919 British colonial rule was set up throughout the peninsula

1941 Japanese invaded Malaya, including Sarawak and North Borneo

1948 Tension and fighting followed the British attempt to establish a Malayan Union

1957 Malaya became independent of Britain

1963 Federation of Malaysia formed under Tunku Abdul Rahman

1981 Dr Mahathir bin Mohamed became Prime Minister

1990 National Development Policy set out to make Malaysia fully-industrialized by the year 2020

1994 'Visit Malaysia Year' brought thousands of new visitors to Malaysia

1998 Malaysia hosts the Commonwealth Games

Index